Germany

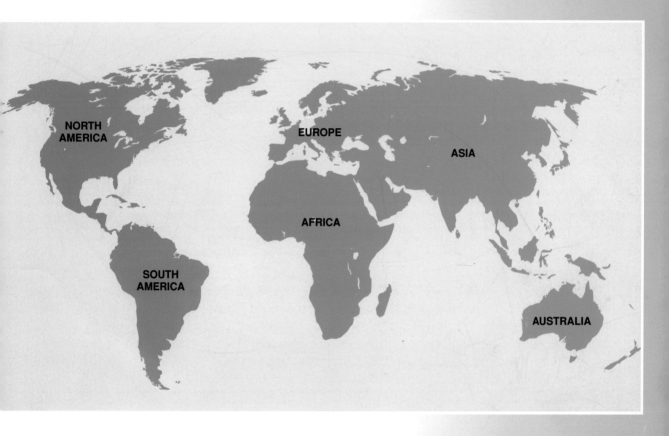

Clare Boast

Heinemann Interactive Library
Des Plaines, Illinois

Published by Heinemann Interactive Library,
an imprint of Reed Educational & Professional Publishing,
1350 East Touhy Avenue, Suit 240 West, Des Plaines, IL 60018

Produced by Times Offset (M) Sdn. Bhd.
Designed by AMR
Illustrations by Art Construction

02 01 00 99 98
10 9 8 7 6 5 4 3 2 1

Boast, Clare, 1965–
    Germany/Clare Boast
        p.   cm. – – (Next stop!)
    Includes bibliographical references and index.
    Summary: An introduction to the history, geography, culture and modern daily life in Germany.
    ISBN 1-57572-566-5
    1. Germany – – Juvenile literature.   [1. Germany.]   I. Title.
II. Series.   97-16747
DD17. 7. B63 1998   C IP
943 – – dc21   AC

Acknowledgments
The author and publisher are grateful to the following for permission to reproduce copyright photographs: J. Allan Cash pp.7, 8; Art Directors p.4; Trevor Clifford pp.10, 12–13, 16–17, 25; Colorific! Reinhard Janke/focus p.27, Alon Reininger/Contact p.18, Peter Turnley/Black Star p.28, Michael Yamashita p.24; Robert Harding Picture Library p.11; Katz Pictures Nascimento/Rea p.15, Tom Stoddart p.5; Spectrum Colour Library p.29; Trip David Cumming pp.14, 19, 22, Eric Smith p.26, R Styles p.6; A Tovy p.9, Trip p.23.

Cover photograph reproduced with permission of:
    background: Tony Stone Images, Stephen Studd
    child: Image Bank.

Special thanks to Betty Root for her comments in the preparation of this book.

Words in the book in bold, **like this**, are explained in the glossary on page 31.

CONTENTS

INTRODUCTION

There are many old castles in Bavaria, an area in the south of Germany.

WHERE IS GERMANY?

Germany is in the middle of Europe. It has borders with nine other countries. It has coastlines on the North Sea and the Baltic Sea.

GERMANY'S HISTORY

Germany was part of the **Roman Empire** for about 500 years. After that, it divided into many smaller countries, but became one country again. After World War II, in 1949, Germany was divided into two countries, East Germany and West Germany. The old capital city, Berlin, was split. In 1961, a concrete wall was built across the city where it was divided.

*Pieces of the Berlin Wall are sold as **souvenirs**. Many **tourists** want a piece of the wall that split Berlin.*

Many common people took part in pulling down the Berlin Wall in 1989.

People in East Germany and West Germany led different lives. People had more money in West Germany than in East Germany. The wall was knocked down in 1989. In 1990, East and West Germany became one country. But it will take some time before everyone has the same chance of a good way of life.

THE LAND

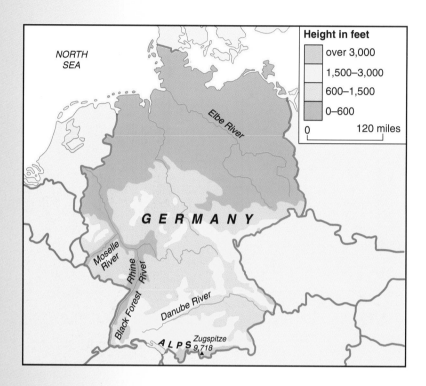

Height in feet

	over 3,000
	1,500–3,000
	600–1,500
	0–600

0   120 miles

NORTH SEA

Elbe River

GERMANY

Moselle River

Rhine River

Black Forest

Danube River

ALPS Zugspitze 9,718

PLAINS

The north of Germany is a large **plain**. It has some low hills and valleys made by rivers that run to the North Sea. The soil is very good for farming.

The Moselle River has carved out a steep-sided valley here.

The plains are very flat in places. Farmers can use big farm machines to cut the wheat.

PLATEAU LAND

The middle of Germany has areas of **plateau** land, broken up by mountains. Some of these mountains are made from the **lava** of old **volcanoes**.

MOUNTAINS

The south of Germany has many mountains. The highest mountains are in the far south. They are the Alps. They separate Germany from other countries.

The highest place in Germany is on top of Zugspitze mountain in the Alps. It is almost 10,000 feet high.

WEATHER, PLANTS, AND ANIMALS

In summer, Berlin is sunny and warm. But in winter, temperatures can be well below freezing.

THE WEATHER

All over Germany people have to be prepared for warm summers and cold winters, especially when the wind blows from the north and east.

Different parts of Germany have different weather. The mountains in the south are always colder and wetter than the low flat plains in the north.

PLANTS AND ANIMALS

Nearly a third of Germany is covered with forests. High in the mountains, there are fir trees. Further down, oak and maple trees grow. Most flat land has been cleared for farming or factories. But there are open areas where the soil is not rich enough for things to grow.

Some mountain areas have been made into **national parks**. Wild boar and deer live there. Foxes and badgers live all over Germany.

Germany has many forests, but lots of the trees are being killed by acid rain. This is rain that is polluted by the smoke from factories.

The Black Forest gets its name from the dark fir trees that grow there.

TOWNS AND CITIES

There has been a town at this place on the Danube River for more than 2,000 years.

Many German towns have old centers. These towns have grown steadily as new houses, factories, and offices are built.

BERLIN

After 1949, Bonn became the capital city of West Germany and East Berlin was the capital of East Germany. Berlin will again be the capital of the unified Germany in the year 2000. Until then, Bonn is the capital city.

TOURISM AND INDUSTRY

Different German towns have grown for different reasons. The area known as the Ruhr has many towns. They are almost joined together with many mines and factories. Other towns are busy ports, like Hamburg. Then there are the **tourist** towns, like the old town of Nuremberg.

There is a toy fair in Nuremberg each year. People from all over the world come to it.

The center of Nuremberg has a special Christmas market. Crowds of people come from all around every year.

LIVING IN STUTTGART

THE BERGER FAMILY

Markus and Heike Berger live in an apartment on the edge of the city of Stuttgart. They have six-year-old twin girls, Ruth and Hannah, and a boy, Jonathan, who is one.

The family lives on the top floor.

Heike cycles to many places with Jonathan.

THE FAMILY'S DAY

Markus runs a nearby factory. Heike runs the household and looks after the children.

The twins go to a local school all day, but they come home for lunch.

These stores are near the family's apartment.

The family eats their evening meal together. They are eating spaghetti and meat sauce.

MEALTIMES

The family eats together most evenings. They like all kinds of different food. Heike has plenty of time to shop and cook, although she needs to be home to make lunch for the twins.

Markus's factory is close enough for him to ride his bike to work.

TIME OFF

The family likes to go for bicycle rides. They are close to the country, because they live in a **suburb**, on the edge of Stuttgart.

Heike takes the car to the supermarket to get a lot of food in one trip.

FARMING IN GERMANY

Germany is a rich country because of its industries. Not many people work in farming. About 70 percent of German farms are too small to make a profit. Farming will only make money if the small farms join up to make larger ones.

SPECIAL CROPS

Some farmers grow just one crop. For example, some farmers grow grapes used in making wine and some farmers grow hops for making beer.

Grapes are grown in vineyards. Grapes can grow in places that are too steep for other crops. But they need warm, sunny weather.

Potato harvesting on a farm in the east of Germany.

OTHER FARMS

Many smaller farms grow crops and raise animals too. They keep cows, sheep, pigs, and chickens. They grow fruit like plums, apples, and pears.

FARMS IN THE NORTH

The best land for farming is on the flat **plains** in the north of Germany. The weather and soil are good for farming. The farms there are the biggest and most profitable. They mainly grow wheat, barley, oats, and potatoes.

Before Germany became one country, the farms in East Germany were run by the government. Now people run their own farms.

15

LIVING IN THE COUNTRY

THE GAISBAUER FAMILY

Hans and Gisela Gaisbauer live in a house on the edge of the town of Passau, in the south of Germany. Passau is near a big forest.

Hans and Gisela have two girls, Ute, who is thirteen, and Almut, eight. They have one boy, Felix, who is eleven.

Hans at work in the forest, looking after the trees.

Ute is learning to play the recorder.

Gisela does most of her shopping on a weekly trip to Passau.

The family is eating their evening meal of fried meat in breadcrumbs, mashed potatoes, and salad.

The children have a big yard where they keep their rabbits.

THE FAMILY'S DAY

Hans is a forest ranger. He works in the nearby forest, clearing away old and fallen trees, looking after young trees, and planting new ones.

Gisela works part-time at a local school. The children go to school. German schools run from 8:00 A.M. to 1:00 P.M. There is always homework.

MEALTIMES

The family eats breakfast together in the morning. They eat their main meal in the evening. They eat bread, meat, and vegetables. A favorite meal is meat loaf with potato dumplings.

Felix and Almut go to school by bus. Ute can walk to her school.

GERMAN STORES

A shopping mall in Hamburg. Many towns and cities have covered shopping malls.

BIG STORES

Germany is a rich country with lots of stores. There are fewer small stores selling one thing, and more big stores selling lots of things. Even people who live near small stores like to drive to a supermarket for their shopping.

Huge supermarkets, called hypermarkets, are on the edges of towns, with lots of parking space for cars.

Cars and buses are not allowed to drive through this pedestrians-only area in Cologne.

SPECIAL STORES

Some small stores have managed to stay open by selling special things. Some just sell cheese, with special types that supermarkets do not sell.

PEDESTRIANS ONLY

Many cities have pedestrians-only areas where cars and buses are not allowed. People can walk around the stores and there is more space for outdoor cafés and small stalls. It is safer and there is less **pollution**, too.

German stores do not use throwaway plastic bags. Many stores also let you return packaging material for recycling.

GERMAN FOOD

TRADITIONAL FOOD

Different parts of Germany have different traditional foods. These foods are usually found locally. So, areas near the sea have lots of fish recipes, like fish soup from Hamburg. There are many different sausages. Frankfurters are a sausage that used to be made just in Frankfurt. Now they are eaten as hot dogs all over the world.

People make traditional food with local fish, meat, and vegetables like these.

Bread is eaten with almost every meal. There are about 300 different types of bread available in Germany.

MEAT AND VEGETABLES

Germans eat more meat, on average, than people in most other countries. German sausages are famous. You can buy them to cook at home. You can also buy them already cooked and spiced, like salami.

People do not eat just meat. Potatoes and green vegetables are eaten almost every day. Cabbage is eaten fresh or pickled with vinegar and spices, called sauerkraut.

German breads are made with many different kinds of flour. Some bread is flavored or is topped with seeds.

MADE IN GERMANY

Germany is a very industrialized country. This means it has a lot of factories that make things. German factories make iron, steel, and chemicals or **goods**—like cars, washing machines, microwave ovens, and CD players.

Germany sells a lot of these goods to other countries. Goods sold to other countries are called **exports**.

This mine in the west of Germany is mining brown coal. This coal is burned to make electricity.

These robots are making **BMW** cars. German factories use the newest ideas and ways of working.

POLLUTION

Pollution is a big problem in Germany. This is partly because there are so many factories. It is also because some factories, especially in what was East Germany, did not use to care about making pollution. But people now realize there is a problem and are trying to modernize the factories and clean up the pollution.

Germany mines more brown coal than any other country in the world.

GETTING AROUND

Germany has a very good system of roads, railroads, and waterways for getting around the country. Most of the big cities have airports, too.

ROADS

German autobahns were the first ever big highways. The first one was built over 50 years ago, and they have been added to ever since. There are no speed limits on these super highways. People can drive as fast as they like.

An autobahn near Berlin. Most people and goods are moved around the country by road.

Trams in Stuttgart run on rails on the road. They have their own routes and stops, just like buses.

TRAINS AND BOATS

All the big cities are linked by high speed trains. The fastest of these travels at about 170 miles per hour. You can get to smaller places on slower trains.

There are many rivers and **canals** in Germany that are used to move goods and people around. They link towns and cities with the sea.

Most cities have good bus and tram services. Big cities, like Berlin and Munich, have their own subway systems.

SPORTS AND VACATIONS

SPORTS

Many people in Germany enjoy watching and playing sport, especially soccer, tennis, track and field, sailing, and skiing. Some people enjoy newer sports, like hang gliding or sailboarding.

PARKS

Germany has many parks with hiking trails and sports fields. There are playgrounds for the children, too. Some parks are built on land where factories used to be.

A hang glider's view of Bavaria. Mountain air currents are good for hang gliding.

TIME OFF

Some people who live in the cities like to go to the country for the weekend. Others prefer to stay in the city, visiting the stores, museums, bars, and cafés.

VACATIONS

Many Germans go to other countries for their vacations. But they might also go to different parts of Germany. They can go skiing in the mountains, or camping in the forests. They can also go to the beaches on the **coast**.

Germany's soccer team has won the World Cup three times.

Soccer fans at an important game in Berlin.

FESTIVALS AND ARTS

The Munich Beer Festival celebrates harvest time.

FESTIVALS

Some German festivals, like Christmas and Easter, are religious. Germany began the tradition of Christmas trees.

Germany has many festivals that are not religious. Some of them celebrate harvest time. The Octoberfest in Munich is a big festival. It is also called the Beer Festival. Hops and barley for beer are important local crops. People come to it from all over the world.

ARTS

Many German music composers are famous. Bach, Beethoven, and Wagner were all German composers. German orchestras and choirs perform all over the world. Many German artists are famous, too. Hans Holbein, who lived in the 1500s, went to England from Germany to paint royalty and rich people.

Many of the fairy tales that we are told, like *Rumplestiltskin* and *Hansel and Gretel*, were retold by the Grimm brothers, who were German.

This is the Children's Festival in the town of Dinkelsbürg. People dress in traditional clothes and dance in the street.

Decorating Christmas trees with lights is a custom that comes from Germany.

GERMANY FACT FILE

People
People from Germany are called Germans.

Capital city
From 2000, the capital city of Germany will be Berlin.

Largest cities
Berlin is the largest city in Germany, with nearly three million people. The second largest city is Hamburg, and Munich is the third largest city.

Head of country
Germany is ruled by a president and a government. The head of the government is called the chancellor.

Population
There are 82 million people living in Germany.

Money
The money in Germany is called the Deutschmark.

Language
People in Germany speak German.

Religion
Most people in Germany are either Protestant or Catholic.

MORE BOOKS TO READ

Ayer, Eleanor H. *Germany: In the Heartland of Europe.* Tarrytown, NY: Marshall Cavendish, 1995.
Phillpotts, Beatrice. *Germany.* Morristown, NJ: Silver Burdett, 1989.

GLOSSARY

canal This is a manmade waterway.

coast This is where the land meets the sea.

exports These are things that are sold to other countries.

goods These are things that people have made.

government This is the people who run the country. In Germany the government is elected by the people.

lava This is melted rock from a volcano.

national park This is an area of land set aside by the government to protect the animals and plants.

plains These are large areas of flat land.

plateau This is a high, flat area of land.

pollution This is dirty air, water, or land.

Roman Empire The Romans were people from Rome in Italy, who took over much of Europe and other parts of the world from about 750 B.C. to 300 A.D.

souvenir This is something that reminds someone of a place they have visited.

suburbs These are smaller towns connected to a large city.

tourist This is someone who visits a place on a vacation.

volcano This is a mountain that sometimes throws out melted rock or ash.

INDEX